summersdale

A LITTLE BIT OF BRIT WIT

Summersdale Publishers Ltd
46 West Street
Chichester
West Sussex
PO19 1RP
UK

www.summersdale.com

Printed and bound in Great Britain

ISBN: 978-1-84953-007-1

Disclaimer
Every effort has been made to attribute the quotations in this collection to the correct source. Should there be any omissions or errors in this respect we apologise and shall be pleased to make the appropriate acknowledgements in any future edition.

Substantial discounts on bulk quantities of Summersdale books are available to corporations, professional associations and other organisations. For details telephone Summersdale Publishers on (+44-1243-771107), fax (+44-1243-786300) or email (nicky@summersdale.com).

A LITTLE BIT OF
Brit Wit

TOM HAY

Contents

Editor's Note

From the best-selling *Brit Wit* books comes the small islander's essential pocket guide to taking the world with a pinch of salt.

Wow your friends, cow your enemies and force yourself to see the funny side in a world that takes itself too seriously and not seriously enough. After all, as Arnold Bax once observed, 'You should make a point of trying every experience once, excepting incest and folk-dancing.'

Whether you're a lover of language or simply want to impress, there are occasions galore when an amusing quip is worth its weight in gold. After all, as Samuel Butler wisely said, 'The principal business of life is to enjoy it.'

Little Britain

I like the English. They
have the most rigid code of
immorality in the world.

Malcolm Bradbury

What two ideas are more
inseparable than Beer
and Britannia?

Revd Sydney Smith

This island is made mainly of coal and surrounded by fish. Only an organising genius could produce a shortage of coal and fish at the same time.

Aneurin Bevan

The Welsh are so damn Welsh
that it looks like affectation.

Alexander Raleigh

The Irish are hearty, the Scotch plausible, the French polite, the Germans good-natured, the Italians courtly, the Spaniards reserved and decorous – the English alone seem to exist in taking and giving offense.

William Hazlitt

Dialect words – those terrible marks of the beast to the truly genteel.
Thomas Hardy

You have to give this much to the Luftwaffe – when it knocked down our buildings it didn't replace them with anything more offensive than rubble. We did that.

Prince Charles

The English Winter – ending
in July to recommence
in August.

Lord Byron

There are still parts of Wales
where the only concession to
gaiety is a striped shroud.

Gwyn Thomas

Bugger Bognor!

King George V

Oats. A grain, which in England is generally given to horses, but in Scotland supports the people.

Samuel Johnson

Ingenious Insults

What a tiresome, affected sod.

Noël Coward on Oscar Wilde

He is morally insensitive and
aesthetically disgusting.

**George Orwell on
Rudyard Kipling**

I regard you with an
indifference bordering
on aversion.

Robert Louis Stevenson

O, she is the antidote
to desire.

William Congreve, *The Way of*
the World

Thou eunuch of language… thou pimp of gender… murderous accoucheur of infant learning… thou pickle-herring in the puppet show of nonsense.

Robert Burns on a critic

The work of a queasy
undergraduate scratching
his pimples.

**Virginia Woolf on *Ulysses* by
James Joyce**

Unreconstructed wankers.

Tony Blair on the Scottish media

❈

Sir, you are like a pin, but
without either its head
or its point.

**Douglas Jerrold to a man who
was boring him**

❈

When they circumcised
Herbert Samuel they threw
away the wrong bit.

David Lloyd George

Lord Sandwich: Sir, you will die either of the pox or on the gallows.

John Wilkes: Depending on whether I embrace your mistress or your principles.

Like the British Constitution, she owes her success in practice to her inconsistencies in principle.

Thomas Hardy, *The Hand of Ethelberta*

Bangers 'n' Mash

I can resist everything except
temptation.

Oscar Wilde,
Lady Windermere's Fan

The secret of a successful restaurant is sharp knives.

George Orwell

Heaven sends us good meat,
but the Devil sends cooks.

David Garrick

Music with dinner is an insult
both to the cook and
the violinist.

G. K. Chesterton

Good apple pies are a
considerable part of our
domestic happiness.

Jane Austen

All happiness depends on a
leisurely breakfast.

John Gunther

My advice if you insist on slimming: eat as much as you like – just don't swallow.

Harry Secombe

There are two types of
women in this world – those
who like chocolate and
complete bitches.

Dawn French

Vegetarianism is harmless
enough, though it is apt to fill
a man with wind and
self-righteousness.

Robert Hutchinson

The salmon are striking back.

**The Queen Mother when choking
on a fish bone**

Life's too short to stuff
a mushroom.

Shirley Conran, *Superwoman*

I Drink, Therefore I Am

A good local pub has much
in common with a church,
except that a pub is warmer,
and there's more conversation.

William Blake

A tavern is a place where madness is sold by the bottle.

Jonathan Swift

Coffee in England always
tastes like a chemistry
experiment.

Agatha Christie

Claret is the liquor for boys; port for men; but he who aspires to be a hero… must drink brandy.

A. E. Housman

This is one of the
disadvantages of wine; it
makes a man mistake words
for thoughts.

Samuel Johnson

And wine can of their wits the
wise beguile,
Make the sage frolic, and the
serious smile.

Alexander Pope

Never drink black coffee at lunch; it will keep you awake all afternoon.

Jilly Cooper

Alcohol is the anesthesia
by which we endure the
operation of life.
George Bernard Shaw

I've stopped drinking, but only while I'm asleep.

George Best

An alcoholic is anyone you
don't like who drinks as much
as you do.

Dylan Thomas

If the headache would only
precede the intoxication,
alcoholism would be a virtue.

Samuel Butler

The Meaning of Life

Drama is life with the dull bits
cut out.

Alfred Hitchcock

The life of every man is a diary
in which he means to write
one story, and writes another.

J. M. Barrie

All animals, except man, know
that the principal business of
life is to enjoy it.

Samuel Butler

Don't be afraid to take big
steps. You can't cross a chasm
in two small jumps.

David Lloyd George

❦

Life is as tedious as a twice-
told tale
Vexing the dull ear of a
drowsy man.

William Shakespeare, *King John*

❦

Man alone is born crying,
lives complaining, and dies
disappointed.

Samuel Johnson

The older one grows, the
more one likes indecency.

Virginia Woolf

We make a living by what
we get, but we make a life by
what we give.

Winston Churchill

It is always the best policy to
tell the truth, unless, of course,
you are an exceptionally
good liar.

Jerome K. Jerome

If you can't be a good example, then you'll just have to be a horrible warning.

Catherine Aird

You should make a point of trying every experience once, excepting incest and folk-dancing.

Arnold Bax

To Have and To Hold

The way to tell if a man is
sexually excited is if
he's breathing.

Jo Brand

The important thing in acting is to be able to laugh and cry. If I have to cry, I think of my sex life. If I have to laugh, I think of my sex life.

Glenda Jackson

Absence – that common cure
of love.

Lord Byron

Bachelors have consciences,
married men have wives.

Samuel Johnson

Maids want nothing but husbands, and when they have them, they want everything.

William Shakespeare

❦

Marriage may often be a
stormy lake, but celibacy is
almost always a muddy
horse pond.

Thomas Love Peacock

❦

Marriage is the result of the longing for the deep, deep peace of the double bed after the hurly-burly of the chaise-longue.

Mrs Patrick Campbell

❭❛❬

Marriage is a wonderful
invention. But, then again, so
is the bicycle repair kit.

Billy Connolly

❭❛❬

The most happy marriage I
can imagine to myself would
be the union of a deaf man to
a blind woman.

Samuel Taylor Coleridge

We invite people like that to tea, but we don't marry them.

Lady Chetwode on her future son-in-law John Betjeman

Men always want to be a woman's first love – women like to be a man's last romance.

Oscar Wilde, *A Woman of No Importance*

Pun In the Work Place

Civil servants – no longer
servants, no longer civil.

Winston Churchill

Well, we can't stand around
here doing nothing. People
will think we're workmen.

Spike Milligan

I like work: it fascinates me. I can sit and look at it for hours.

Jerome K. Jerome

Make lots of money. Enjoy the work. Operate within the law. Choose any two of three.

Jack Dee

❦

Idleness is only a coarse name
for my infinite capacity for
living in the present.
Cyril Connolly

❦

Every man is a potential
genius until he does
something.

Herbert Beerbohm Tree

If you can't get a job as a pianist in a brothel you become a royal reporter.

Max Hastings

If at first you don't succeed,
failure may be your style.

Quentin Crisp

Nothing is really work unless
you would rather be doing
something else.

J. M. Barrie

Work is not always required.
There is such a thing as
sacred idleness.

George MacDonald

Dark forces dragged me away from the keyboard, swirling forces of irresistible intensity and power.

Boris Johnson's excuse for missing a deadline

Johnny Foreigner

Abroad is unutterably bloody
and foreigners are fiends.

**Nancy Mitford, *The Pursuit
of Love***

The best thing I know
between France and England
is the sea.

**Douglas Jerrold on the Anglo-
French Alliance**

We have really everything
in common with America
nowadays except, of course,
language.

**Oscar Wilde, *The Canterville
Ghost***

I look upon Switzerland as an inferior sort of Scotland.

Revd Sydney Smith

I don't hold with abroad and
think that foreigners speak
English when our backs
are turned.

Quentin Crisp

❦

That kind of patriotism which consists in hating all other nations.

Mrs Gaskell, *Sylvia's Lovers*

❦

You can always count on
Americans to do the right
thing – after they've tried
everything else.

Winston Churchill

I grew up in Europe, where
the history comes from.

Eddie Izzard

Los Angeles is awful – like
Liverpool with palm trees.

Johnny Rotten

The British tourist is always happy abroad as long as the natives are waiters.

Robert Morley

The proper means of
increasing the love we bear
our native country is to reside
some time in a foreign one.

William Shenstone

A Non-prophet
Organisation

What would I like the sermon
to be about, vicar? I would like
it to be about ten minutes.

Arthur Wellesley

❰•❱

When did I realise I was God?
Well, I was praying and I
suddenly realised I was talking
to myself.

Peter O'Toole

❰•❱

There is no sinner like a
young saint.

Aphra Behn

---•◆•---

The Bible tells us to love
our neighbours, and also to
love our enemies; probably
because generally they are the
same people.

G. K. Chesterton

---•◆•---

Faith goes out through the window when beauty comes in at the door.

George Moore

When the gods want to
punish us, they answer
our prayers.
Oscar Wilde

The New Testament is basically about what happened when God got religion.

Terry Pratchett

To the philosophical eye the vices of the clergy are far less dangerous than their virtues.

Edward Gibbon, *The Decline and Fall of the Roman Empire*

Heresy is another word for
freedom of thought.

Graham Greene

Religion to me has always
been the wound, not
the bandage.
Dennis Potter

God is a gentleman. He
prefers blondes.

Joe Orton, *Loot*

Resistance Is Feudal

The best argument against democracy is a five minute conversation with the average voter.

Winston Churchill

No man is regular in his
attendance at the House of
Commons until he is married.

Benjamin Disraeli

— ✦ —

In politics, if you want
anything said, ask a man. If
you want something done,
ask a woman.

Margaret Thatcher

— ✦ —

She can't see an institution
without hitting it with
her handbag.

**Julian Critchley on Margaret
Thatcher**

The Labour Party's election
manifesto is the longest
suicide note in history.

Greg Knight

Politics are usually the executive expression of human immaturity.

Vera Brittain

A foreign secretary is forever
poised between the cliché and
the indiscretion.

Harold MacMillan

Tony Blair puts two poems in
a bus shelter and calls it
a university.

Victoria Wood

A parliament is nothing less
than a big meeting of more or
less idle people.

Walter Bagehot

The proper memory for a politician is one that knows what to remember and what to forget.

John Morley

The House of Commons is the
longest running farce in
the West End.

Cyril Smith

Be a Sport

In my opinion cricket is too
great a game to think
about statistically.

E. H. Hendren

In 1823, William Webb Ellis first picked up the ball in his arms and ran with it. And for the next 156 years forwards have been trying to work out why.

Tasker Watkins

The Oxford rowing crew –
eight minds with but a single
thought, if that.

Max Beerbohm

I became a great runner
because if you're a kid in
Leeds and your name is
Sebastian you've got to
become a great runner.

Sebastian Coe

Cricket is a game which the British, not being a spiritual people, had to invent in order to have some concept of eternity.

Lord Mancroft

That's great, tell him he's Pelé
and get him back on.

**John Lambie, Partick Thistle
manager, when told a concussed
striker did not know who he was**

I regard golf as an expensive
way of playing marbles.

G. K. Chesterton

Jogging is for people who
aren't intelligent enough to
watch television.

Victoria Wood

I don't make mistakes. I make
prophesies which immediately
turn out to be wrong.

Murray Walker

Golf is a day spent in a round
of strenuous idleness.

William Wordsworth

The only athletic sport I ever
mastered was backgammon.

Douglas Jerrold

The Arts

No opera plot can be sensible,
for in sensible situations
people do not sing.

W. H. Auden

The harpsichord sounds like
two skeletons copulating on a
corrugated iron roof – in
a thunderstorm.

Thomas Beecham

❦

I couldn't warm to Chuck
Berry even if I was cremated
next to him.

Keith Richards

❦

People are wrong when they say that opera is not what it used to be. It is what it used to be. That is what is wrong with it.

Noël Coward

I want to do a musical movie.
Like *Evita*, but with
good music.

Elton John

Somerset Maugham said there were three rules for writing – and nobody knows what they are.

Joan Collins

If Botticelli were alive today
he'd be working for *Vogue*.

Peter Ustinov

I'm a skilled, professional actor.
Whether or not I've any talent
is beside the point.

Michael Caine

❦

Acting is merely the art of
keeping a large group of
people from coughing.
Ralph Richardson

❦

The moral of filmmaking
in Britain is that you will be
screwed by the weather.

Hugh Grant

———— ·❧ ————

Seeing a murder on television
can help work off one's
antagonisms. And if you
haven't any antagonisms, the
commercials will give
you some.

Alfred Hitchcock

———— ·❧ ————

Battle of the Sexes

The first time Adam had the
chance, he put the blame on
a woman.

Nancy Astor

Being a woman is a terribly
difficult task, since it consists
principally in dealing
with men.

Joseph Conrad

The main difference between
men and women is that men
are lunatics and women
are idiots.

Rebecca West

Men at most differ as Heaven and Earth, but women, worst and best, as Heaven and Hell.

Alfred Lord Tennyson

For most of history,
Anonymous was a woman.

Virginia Woolf

In the sex war, thoughtlessness
is the weapon of the male,
vindictiveness of the female.

Cyril Connolly

A man… is so in the way in the house!

Mrs Gaskell

Men are people, just like
women.

Fenella Fielding

Being powerful is like being a lady. If you have to tell people you are, you aren't.

Margaret Thatcher

I'll Tell You This
For Free

A sure cure for seasickness is to
sit under a tree.

Spike Milligan

Don't give a woman advice:
one should never give a
woman anything she can't
wear in the evening.

Oscar Wilde

Never stand so high
upon a principle that you
cannot lower it to suit the
circumstances.

Winston Churchill

Never keep up with the Joneses. Drag them down to your level. It's cheaper.

Quentin Crisp

Have the courage to be
ignorant of a great number of
things, in order to avoid the
calamity of being ignorant
of everything.

Revd Sydney Smith

One should only see a
psychiatrist out of boredom.

Muriel Spark

It's OK to let yourself go, just as long as you let yourself back.

Mick Jagger

A little inaccuracy sometimes
saves tons of explanation.

Saki

❖

Good but rarely came from good advice.

Lord Byron

❖

The worst men often give the best advice.

Francis Bacon

Good advice is always certain to be ignored, but that's no reason not to give it.

Agatha Christie

Have you enjoyed this book? If so, why
not write a review on your
favourite website?

Thanks very much for buying this
Summersdale book.

www.summersdale.com